Killer BEES!

Rob Waring, *Series Editor*

HEINLE
CENGAGE Learning

Australia • Brazil • Japan • Korea • Mexico • Singapore • Spain • United Kingdom • United States

Words to Know

This story is set in Latin America. It happens on the continent of South America, and in the countries of Panama and Mexico.

MEXICO

PANAMA

A **The Central American Rain Forest.** Read the paragraph. Then match each word with the correct definition.

There are many different creatures under the canopy of the Central American rain forest, including butterflies, bats, and bees. This story is about two types, or species, of bees. The first type of bee is native to Panama, so the rain forest is considered its habitat. The other type of bee has come from another country and invaded the Central American rain forest. In the story, an entomologist named David Roubik [rubɪk] studies these bees to see how they are affecting each other.

1. creature _____	**a.** the natural environment where an animal or plant lives
2. canopy _____	**b.** a scientist who studies insects
3. species _____	**c.** a living being capable of independent movement
4. habitat _____	**d.** enter an area uninvited and take control
5. invade _____	**e.** the cover provided by the trees in the upper level of a rain forest
6. entomologist _____	**f.** a specific group of animals or plants that have similar characteristics

B **Native Bees vs. Killer Bees.** Read the facts about bees. Then write the correct form of each underlined word next to the correct definition.

Many bees live in hives.
Native bees in Panama make honey for people to eat.
Native bees help flowers to produce seeds by pollinating them.
Killer bees fly in large swarms of several thousand.
Native bees play an important role in helping plants and flowers to reproduce.

1. produce children, or more plants and flowers: _____
2. a group of insects all moving together: _____
3. a sweet, golden-colored, sticky food: _____
4. structures where bees make their home: _____
5. carry a special powder, called pollen, from one flower to another: _____

a bat

a bee

a butterfly

Creatures of the Rain Forest

For thousands of years, an insect has kept the rain forests of Central America alive. This insect is one of the smallest and least understood creatures on Earth—the bee. Now, a foreign species of bee has invaded these rain forests. One man believes that this foreign bee may cause problems for the whole rain forest. He's ready to take any risk to find out the truth. This man is entomologist David Roubik.

🎧 CD 3, Track 05

Central American Native Bee

Some entomologists really get close to bees!

Roubik loves bees so much that he has spent much of his life studying them. He'll go anywhere to get closer to his favorite creatures. He even drives over rocky and difficult roads to get far into the rain forest.

Roubik has studied bees for over 30 years, so he is one of the world's leading experts on native bees. He works deep in the rain forests of Panama, and there are often swarms of bees right next to him. This has allowed him to become more familiar with them than almost anyone else.

When Roubik talks about the bees and his studies, it's clear that both are very interesting to him. "I've counted more than 300 species of bees in just one small forest area in Panama," he says. "It's just in a **square kilometer**[1]* of forest, but there might be a million or more individual bees!" he adds excitedly.

It's also clear that Panama is the perfect place for Roubik to study the bees. He explains in his own words: "This is really about the best place in the world to do the kind of work that I'm doing. [The bees] **interact**[2] with everything. They pollinate the plants. They provide food for a lot of different animals. They live in the most **outlandish**,[3] interesting places; from the top of the rain forest canopy to holes deep underground. So it's a wonderful group to look at."

---

[1]**square kilometer:** the area of a square with sides of one kilometer
[2]**interact:** come together with and affect
[3]**outlandish:** very strange and unusual
*See page 32 for a metric conversion chart.

Identify the Main Idea

1. What is the main idea in paragraph
   2 on page 8?

2. What are two pieces of information that
   support this idea?

Unfortunately, Roubik thinks that the future of these amazing native bees looks bad. Little by little, people are destroying the rain forest habitat of the bees. People are also responsible for something that Roubik sees as an even more immediate environmental problem. It is a problem that is the direct result of a scientific experiment that went terribly wrong.

In 1957, a group of scientists in the eastern part of South America wanted to improve honey production. To do this, they started studying a bee that was non-native to the area: the African honeybee. The African honeybee is far more **adaptable**[4] than most native species. It's also a bee that can reproduce very quickly. In fact, it's capable of developing larger swarms than other native bee groups in a very short time. However, there's one big disadvantage to working with the African honeybee. If anything bothers it, it can become dangerous— very dangerous!

At first, the study of the African honeybees was proceeding in a completely regular way. Then, one day, some of the honeybees escaped. Something that at first seemed to be a bit of bad luck, eventually became a very costly mistake.

---

[4]**adaptable:** able to change to suit different situations or uses

The hungry African bees spread very quickly throughout South America and were soon known as 'killer bees.' The name was given to them because of their large swarms, angry behavior, and potential to hurt people by **stinging**[5] them repeatedly.

Roubik went to Panama in 1979 to find some answers to the problem of the killer bees. People were worried about how the bees would affect the environment. By 1982, this powerful foreign bee had crossed almost all of the South American continent. It was starting to make its home in Panama. Roubik realized that the life of the rain forest and its native bees were in danger. They would never be the same again. The killer bees had arrived.

---

[5]**sting:** cause pain; if a bee stings something, it puts a pain-causing substance into the skin

Sequence the Events

What is the correct order of the events?
Write numbers.

_____ The killer bee started making its home in Panama.

_____ David Roubik was sent to Panama.

_____ Some of the African honeybees escaped.

_____ Scientists started to study the African honeybee.

1990

1985

1980

1977

Roubik tells how the media reacted to this troubling news. He says that newspapers and television mostly told a terrifying story. They talked only of a group of 'killer bees' that were traveling through South and Central America. He says that they invented this story for excitement, but they didn't really discuss the important story at all.

According to Roubik, the biggest danger was not to man. The real danger was to the future of the rain forests in Latin America. Native bees are pollinators that play an important role in making plants reproduce. Without the native bees, Roubik was worried that the rain forests could not survive. Once the killer bees arrived, things started changing.

The hungry African bees spread quickly throughout South America.

To understand the true effects of the killer bees, Roubik must study them up close. He explains as he examines a beehive of the killer bees, "This is one of the millions," he says pointing to the beehive. "These bees have done something no other bee ever did. These things have **sucked up**[6] most of the resources that are out there for bees—and for other animals, too. [It's] not just bees [that] visit flowers for food. Birds, bats, butterflies … other things take the same food."

Roubik then talks about the size of the problem: "It's not just here and there; it's really everywhere. All the **vast**[7] forest areas we think of as absolute **wildlife preserves**[8] have been **violated**[9] by this bee. This bee doesn't belong in any of them, [but] it lives in all of them. It's not going to go away."

[6]**suck up:** take away quickly
[7]**vast:** wide in area
[8]**wildlife preserve:** a region saved for animals to live in their natural environment
[9]**violate:** enter a private or special place without permission

Roubik may have discovered what the real danger with the invading bee is. It has better skills for finding food and for taking over areas from other animals and bees. Because of its large numbers and strength, the killer bee has little to fear from most creatures. Roubik knows that nothing will likely stop the advance of the killer bees in Central America.

But what about the native bees of Panama? Will they be able to compete with their hungry new neighbors? The sight of native beehives with no native bees in them seems to tell a warning story: there is no honey here. Still, Roubik needs to know for sure, so he goes to a place called Tulum, Mexico.

Tulum is home to the ancient buildings of the Maya, a very old culture from Mexico and Central America. Here, Roubik hopes to find **data**[10] that indicates just how big of a danger the killer bees really are. He wants to prove that the killer bees could seriously hurt the native bees and the rain forests that depend on them.

As he walks among the ancient buildings, Roubik explains why he has made the trip: "My data would only reach back 15 years, but I needed someone with even more experience with native bees. That's what the Maya in particular had to offer." Roubik further explains that the native bee has been an important part of Maya culture for over 1,000 years. If there was any change in the bee population, they would likely know.

[10]**data:** information or facts about something

The **descendants**[11] of the ancient Maya have always kept native bees in the traditional way—until now. Modern-day Maya farmers now believe that the killer bees have caused huge changes. According to Roubik, a few years ago, there used to be a lot of honey in these farmers' hives. In fact, there was so much, that it almost 'jumped out at you,' or came out of the hive when it was opened. "Fifteen years ago, the honey used to jump out at you," says Roubik as he sits next to a farmer's hive. "[Farmers used to] take off the hive cover and there would be honey right out to the edge," he says as he points to the outer edge of the hive.

Things have now changed. "Now I can reach my arm in there and there is just space," explains Roubik as he reaches into the farmer's hive and finds nothing. "These people noticed, in terms of two or three years after the African bees arrived, their native bees and their honey were not there," he adds. Roubik finds the situation very strange and unusual. A part of the Maya culture that lasted for thousands of years has disappeared in just a few years. And it all happened because of man's mistake.

---

[11]**descendant:** born into a certain family line

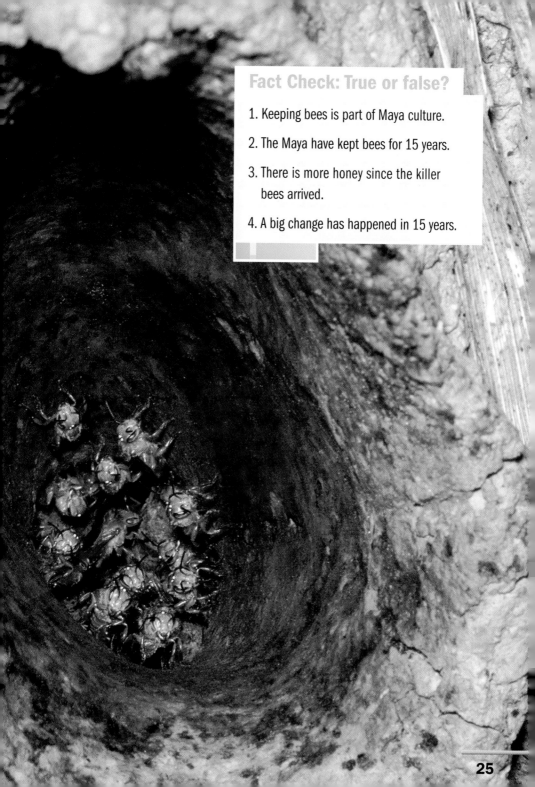

Fact Check: True or false?

1. Keeping bees is part of Maya culture.

2. The Maya have kept bees for 15 years.

3. There is more honey since the killer bees arrived.

4. A big change has happened in 15 years.

Roubik has finally proved an important point—the African bee appears to be forcing out native bees. It's an absolutely terrible discovery for the entomologist. "The **disturbing**[12] reality is that [the African honeybee is] not a natural part of this community," says Roubik. "Yet it has become part of nature, and **ironically**,[13] man has put it there. But man can't take it away," he then adds.

Nobody really knows if the native bees of Latin America will survive, and it may take many years to find out. However, deep in the heart of Panama, Roubik continues his research. He intends to learn more about the secrets of native bee life before it's too late.

---

[12] **disturbing:** emotionally uncomfortable
[13] **ironic:** strange because it is the opposite of what was expected

After You Read

1. This story indicates that one insect has a _____ role in the survival of the rain forest.
   A. small
   B. private
   C. significant
   D. lucky

2. What is the purpose of page 7?
   A. to explain that entomologists love bees
   B. to introduce a strange creature in the rain forest
   C. to show that the rain forest is a dangerous place
   D. to show that Roubik is knowledgeable about bees

3. What view does Roubik express about Panama?
   A. It's a great place to take a vacation.
   B. Bees can be studied easily there.
   C. There are many kinds of plants there.
   D. The rain forest has invaded the bees' habitat.

4. On page 11, the word 'terribly' can be replaced by:
   A. seriously
   B. clearly
   C. immediately
   D. happily

5. Which is a good heading for paragraph 2 on page 12?
   A. Deadly Insect in South America
   B. Bees Kept in Research Area
   C. Small Accident Causes Big Problems
   D. Honeybees Don't Make Honey

6. What role did the media have in the killer bee situation?
   A. They educated others about the insect.
   B. They explained about pollination problems.
   C. They frightened the public.
   D. They said the Roubik was a hero.

7. In paragraph 1 on page 19, 'them' refers to:
   A. people
   B. entomologists
   C. birds
   D. bees

8. The killer bee is not native _____ South America.
   A. in
   B. to
   C. by
   D. of

9. In paragraph 2 on page 20, what does the 'warning story' explain?
   A. that swarms of honeybees will come
   B. that Roubik must visit ancient buildings
   C. that the killer bees have moved to another home
   D. that the native bees are in trouble

10. Each of the following is a good heading for page 23 EXCEPT:
   A. Scientist Travels for Answers
   B. The Maya May Have Information
   C. Over Fifty Years of Data Isn't Enough
   D. Ancient Culture Expert on Native Bees

11. In paragraph 2 on page 24, 'man' refers to:
   A. farmers
   B. humans
   C. the Maya culture
   D. Roubik

12. What does the writer probably think about the bee problem?
   A. The dangerous bees must go back to Africa.
   B. The South American farmers should stop keeping bees.
   C. One mistake has caused great damage.
   D. Roubik should return to his home.

The AMAZING BUTTERFLY

Butterflies are among the most beautiful creatures in the world. They are also one of the most amazing. The female butterfly produces from one hundred to several hundred eggs at a time. She is also extremely careful about where she lays her eggs when she is ready to reproduce. Different butterfly species prefer different species of plants. After choosing a plant, the female tests the surface of several leaves with her feet until she finds one that feels acceptable. Then, she lays her eggs.

Each butterfly starts its life in the form of a 'caterpillar', which doesn't look anything like a butterfly. This soft, round, little creature has lots of very short legs and no wings. As soon as it is born, it becomes an eating machine that eats a lot and often. Caterpillars can grow to 3,000 times their birth weight in just two weeks. Next, the caterpillar creates a special covering and goes into the 'pupal stage'. Some butterflies go through this process under the ground, but many do it while they hang in trees. After a specific period of time, a full-grown butterfly comes out of the covering.

Caterpillar　　　　　　　　**Pupal Stage**

Unusual Butterflies

Name	Colors	Size	Habitat	Unusual Feature
Peacock Butterfly	mostly brown and purple	5 cm wide	Europe and Asia	wings look like bird's face
Goliath Birdwing Butterfly	blue, yellow, and green	28 cm wide	Indonesian rain forests	very large size
American Snout Butterfly	orange and brown	5 cm wide	United States	adult's wings look like dead leaves

Here are some other unusual butterfly facts that entomologists have learned:

- The shiny colors seen on butterfly wings are not actually solid colors. The colors are created by light reflecting off very small scales that cover the creature's wings.

- Butterflies do not eat solid food. They only drink.

- Some butterflies go to different places at certain times each year. The Monarch butterfly of North America flies to the mountains of Mexico each winter.

- The world's fastest butterfly is the Monarch. It can go as fast as 17 miles per hour.

- Many butterflies can stop developing for a period of time if conditions are not right. For example, if the temperature drops very suddenly, a butterfly in the egg or pupal stage will stop developing. When the temperature rises enough, their development will continue.

CD 3, Track 06

Word Count: 329
Time: _____

Vocabulary List

adaptable (12)

bat (2, 3, 19)

bee (2, 3, 4, 6, 7, 8, 11, 12, 14, 15, 17, 19, 20, 23, 24, 25, 27)

butterfly (2, 3, 19)

canopy (2, 8)

creature (2, 3, 4, 7, 20)

data (23)

descendent (24)

disturbing (27)

entomologist (2, 4, 6, 27)

habitat (2, 11)

hive (3, 19, 20, 24)

honey (3, 12, 15, 20, 24, 25, 27)

interact (8)

invade (2, 4, 20)

ironic (27)

outlandish (8)

pollinate (3, 8, 17)

reproduce (3, 12, 17)

species (2, 4, 8, 12)

square kilometer (8)

sting (14)

suck up (19)

swarm (3, 7, 12, 14)

vast (19)

violate (19)

wildlife preserve (19)

Metric Conversion Chart

Area

1 hectare = 2.471 acres

Length

1 centimeter = .394 inches

1 meter = 1.094 yards

1 kilometer = .621 miles

Temperature

0° Celsius = 32° Fahrenheit

Volume

1 liter = 1.057 quarts

Weight

1 gram = .035 ounces

1 kilogram = 2.2 pounds